D1267106

EARTH'S
NATURAL
BIOMES

MARINE

BIOMES

Louise and Richard Spilsbury

 Crabtree Publishing Company
www.crabtreebooks.com

Crabtree Publishing Company
www.crabtreebooks.com
1-800-387-7650

Published in Canada
Crabtree Publishing
616 Welland Avenue
St. Catharines, ON
L2M 5V6

Published in the United States
Crabtree Publishing
PMB 59051
350 Fifth Ave, 59th Floor
New York, NY 10118

Published in 2018 by CRABTREE PUBLISHING COMPANY.

First published in 2017 by Wayland
Copyright © Wayland, 2017

Authors: Louise Spilsbury, Richard Spilsbury

Editors: Hayley Fairhead, Philip Gebhardt

Design: Smart Design Studio

Map (page 6) by Stefan Chabluk

Editorial director: Kathy Middleton

Proofreader: Lorna Notsch

Prepress technician: Tammy McGarr

Print and production coordinator: Margaret Amy Salter

Photographs

All photographs supplied by Nature Picture Library
www.naturepl.com

Front cover(main), title page(b) and p9 Aflo; title page(main) and p28 Michael Pitts; p4 Wim van den Heever; p5 Tui De Roy; p6, front cover(tr) and title page(tr) Klein and Hubert; p7 and contents page(t) Alex Mustard; p8 Jeff Rotman; p10 Georgette Douwma; p11 Laurie Campbell; p12, front cover(br) and contents page(b) Pascal Kobeh; p13 and back cover(tr) Alex Mustard; p14 and p32(b) Roy Mangersnes; p15 Doug Allan; p16 David Shale; p17 Doug Perrine; p18 Franco Banfi; p19 and p31(b) Chris and Monique Fallows; p20 Alex Mustard; p21 and imprint page(t) Pedro Narra; p22 Solvin Zankl / Geomar; p23 and imprint page(b) Tom Mangelsen; p24 and p31(t) Franco Banfi; p25 and back cover(tl) Jose B. Ruiz; p26, front cover(tl) and p32(t) Roland Seitre; p27 Dan Barton; p29 Brandon Cole.

Printed in the USA/122019/BG20171102

Library and Archives Canada Cataloguing in Publication

Spilsbury, Louise, author
    Marine biomes / Louise Spilsbury, Richard Spilsbury.

(Earth's natural biomes)
Includes index.
Issued in print and electronic formats.
ISBN 978-0-7787-3996-8 (hardcover).--
ISBN 978-0-7787-4181-7 (softcover).--
ISBN 978-1-4271-2006-9 (HTML)

    1. Marine ecology--Juvenile literature. 2. Ocean--Juvenile literature. I. Spilsbury, Richard, 1963-, author II. Title.

QH541.5.S3S656 2018   j577.7   C2017-906895-4
                                             C2017-906896-2

Library of Congress Cataloging-in Publication Data

Names: Spilsbury, Louise, author. | Spilsbury, Richard, 1963- author.
Title: Marine biomes / Louise Spilsbury, Richard Spilsbury.
Description: New York, New York : Crabtree Publishing Company, 2018. | Series: Earth's natural biomes | Includes index. |
Identifiers: LCCN 2017051158 (print) | LCCN 2017053956 (ebook) | ISBN 9781427120069 (Electronic HTML) | ISBN 9780778739968 (reinforced library binding) | ISBN 9780778741817 (pbk.)
Subjects: LCSH: Marine ecology--Juvenile literature. | Marine ecological regions--Juvenile literature. | Marine resources conservation--Juvenile literature.
Classification: LCC QH541.5.S3 (ebook) | LCC QH541.5.S3 S6554 2018 (print) | DDC 577.7--dc23
LC record available at https://lccn.loc.gov/2017051158

CONTENTS

WHAT ARE MARINE BIOMES?

Marine **biomes** cover about three-quarters of Earth's surface. They include open ocean water, the world's coastlines and seashores, colorful coral reefs, the mysterious hidden world of the deep, dark oceans, and the seabed.

Ocean challenges

Marine biomes are challenging places for plants and animals to live. The salt in seawater would dry out and kill most living things if they drank a lot of it. Winds across the water's surface whip up high waves that can be rough and powerful. In places, oceans reach incredible depths, and the deeper it gets the darker and colder it becomes.

Marine biomes are home to many different animals, such as these bottlenose dolphins surfing high waves in waters off South Africa.

Amazing Adaptation

Adaptations are special features or body parts that living things develop over time to help them survive in a biome. Sea lions and dolphins have strong, paddle-like **flippers** to help them swim and a long, narrow body shape to cut through waves.

Ocean survival

In spite of these challenges, the marine biome is full of life. **Plankton** consists of tiny plants and animals so small they cannot be seen without a microscope, but there can be over a million plankton in just a quart (liter) of seawater! In contrast, some types of **seaweed** can be up to 100 feet (30 m) long.

There is a huge variety of marine animals. Some, such as fish, live, breathe, feed, and have their young in the ocean without ever leaving the water. Others, including the millions of sea birds that fly over the water searching for fish, only visit the ocean biome to catch food.

Some animals, such as sea lions, live mainly in seawater, but come to the surface to breathe or go ashore to rest and have their young.

Fact Focus: Biome or Habitat?

Biomes are regions of the world, such as deserts, forests, rivers, oceans, tundra and grassland, that have a similar **climate**, plants, and animals. **A habitat** is the specific place in a biome where a plant or animal lives.

MARINE BIOMES OF THE WORLD

There are five oceans in the world. They are all connected and water flows between them. Within these marine biomes, there are also seas, which are smaller areas of an ocean that are usually partly surrounded by land.

The Arctic Ocean

The Arctic Ocean covers the area around the North Pole. This ocean is the smallest in the world. It is so cold that its center is permanently covered with ice 10 feet (3 m) thick. In summer, the edges of the ocean melt.

The Southern Ocean

The Southern, or Antarctic, Ocean, surrounds the **continent** of Antarctica. In winter, the water around the edges of Antarctica freezes. In summer, it melts again. It includes several seas, such as the huge Weddell Sea.

Adelie penguins dive off Antarctic ice into the Southern Ocean to catch food, such as shrimp–like krill. (See page 22.)

The oceans are mostly separated by the seven continents, except for the Southern Ocean, which runs into other oceans.

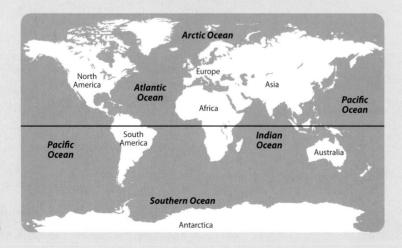

Arctic Ocean

North America

Europe

Asia

Atlantic Ocean

Africa

Pacific Ocean

Pacific Ocean

South America

Indian Ocean

Australia

Southern Ocean

Antarctica

The Indian Ocean

The Indian Ocean is the warmest on Earth because a large part of it lies in the **tropics**. Some of the Indian Ocean's surface water is as hot as a warm bath!

The Atlantic Ocean

The Atlantic Ocean is the second largest ocean on Earth. It is warmer near the **equator** and colder in the far north and south. The Atlantic includes seas, such as the North Sea and the Caribbean Sea.

The Pacific Ocean

The Pacific Ocean is the largest of the five oceans. Where it meets the Southern Ocean, its waters are freezing cold, but near the equator, its waters are much warmer.

Amazing Adaptation

The hammerhead shark's eyes are at the ends of its hammer-shaped head, so it can see all around when looking for **prey**.

Hammerhead sharks live in the Pacific, Atlantic and the Indian oceans.

LIVING UNDERWATER

Living underwater is hard work! Two major challenges facing living things are finding oxygen to breathe and drinking salty seawater.

Breathing

Seaweed, a plant-like **algae** growing in marine biomes, releases oxygen into seawater as part of the **photosynthesis** process. Most living things need to take in oxygen to survive. Fish breathe underwater by using their **gills**. Some fish gulp water into their mouth and pump it over the gills. Oxygen **dissolved** in seawater passes into the gills and the fish's body. Other fish force water past their gills as they swim forward with their mouths open.

The sand tiger shark has five large gill slits on each side of its pointed head. It can breathe while still or moving.

Surviving the salt

Some marine animals, such as sea otters, have extra-large **kidneys**. These **organs** work hard to remove the salt from seawater and eliminate it in the animal's **urine**. The sea turtle empties salt from its body through its eyes—and looks like it's crying as it does so!

On the move

An animal can be slowed down by **friction** between its body and the water. That's why many marine animals are a long, narrow, **streamlined** shape. This reduces the area at the front of their body pushing against the water, so they can move more quickly. Fish, dolphins, and whales move their tails up and down to swim and dive. Fins help them to steer, brake, and balance. Some animals have flippers or webbed feet to push against the water.

Other animals move by jet propulsion! Octopus, squid, and some jellyfish open out the bell-shaped top part of their body and fill it with water. Then they squeeze it tight to push the water out. The push of the water moves them forwards.

As a sea nettle jellyfish swims along, its long **tentacles** stun fish and other prey that brush against it. The tentacles then drag prey into its mouth.

Amazing Adaptation

Most fish have a gas-filled bag called a swim bladder just below their backbone. The swim bladder fills with air to help fish float and releases air, so fish can sink and dive.

COASTS

Coasts are constantly changing. Powerful waves crash into the land and rising and falling **tides** cover a shore with seawater, then expose them to harsh wind and hot sun.

Super seaweed

A large breaking wave is strong enough to shift rocks and move piles of sand along a beach. The rubbery types of seaweed that live near the coast have parts called **holdfasts** that hold them tightly to rocks. They also have leaf-like parts called **fronds** that are flexible and bend with the waves, so they don't get broken as they float in the water. Many seaweeds are covered in slime that prevents drying out when the tide goes out.

Amazing Adaptation

Many types of seaweed have air-filled pockets along their fronds that help them float near the surface. This allows them to capture the Sun's energy to make food through photosynthesis.

Kelp is a giant seaweed that can form large underwater forests. It has huge holdfasts to anchor it to the ocean floor.

Saved by the shell

The soft bodies of many coastal animals are covered in shells. **Mollusks**, such as limpets and barnacles, have a muscular foot that sucks tightly onto rocks. They hide beneath hard, cone-shaped shells so waves don't wash them away. At low tide, their shells prevent the Sun and wind from drying them out. Hard shells also protect animals, such as crabs, from some of the birds, fish, and other **predators** that try to eat them.

Hide and seek

Another way to escape harsh winds, drying Sun, strong waves, and predators is to hide under the sand! Sand mason worms are about 12 inches (30 cm) long. They live under the sand, but build a tube using bits of shell, mud, and sand cemented together with mucus. The tube sticks out above the sand's surface. They use the tube to keep safe when they come out of the sand to capture plankton from the water to eat.

Tentacles

A sand mason worm captures food using tentacles that sprout from its head. The top of the tube is shaped to support the finger-like tentacles when they are stretched out.

CORAL REEFS

Coral reefs are the most colorful habitats in the marine biome. These rocky structures form in fairly shallow water in warm oceans and provide food and shelter to many different animals. They can be enormous, but they are built by tiny creatures called coral polyps.

Amazing Adaptation

Giant moray eels are about 10 feet (3 m) long and have long, thin bodies, which can squeeze into cracks in the reef. They hide here until they smell prey. Then they dart out and catch it.

Moray eels come out of their coral reef caves to grab slippery prey, such as fish and octopus, in their large, sharp teeth.

Coral construction

Coral polyps are like tiny, soft-bodied animals. They take calcium from seawater to help them build cup-shaped cases of **limestone** to protect their soft bodies. Over time, thousands of these stony cases grow together to form coral reefs. The polyps living inside only stretch out their tiny tentacles to feed at night. Plant-like algae live among corals, as well as animals, such as sea stars and moray eels.

Fishing on the reefs

The teeth of parrotfish are fused together to form a sort of beak that can chip off pieces of coral to eat. Angelfish have long snouts and sharp teeth that they poke into small gaps to graze on the algae there.

Clownfish have a unique relationship with sea anemones. Sea anemones live in one place and catch small shrimp and fish with their poisonous tentacles. A clownfish is too big for the anemone to eat and is unaffected by the anemone's deadly stings. It lives among the tentacles, safe from predators, and feeds on damaged tentacles and tiny animals that could harm the anemone.

The sea anemone provides safe shelter for the clownfish, which in turn protects the sea anemone from pests.

Fact File: The Great Barrier Reef

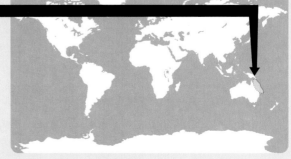

Location: Northeast coast of Australia
Size: Over 1,250 miles (2,000 km) long
Overview: The biggest coral reef in the world—it can be seen from the Moon! It has many different colored corals and animals, such as sea turtles and dolphins.

FROZEN OCEANS

Few animals can survive the icy waters near the North and South Poles. The water here is bitterly cold, and it's often frozen into a layer of solid ice at the surface. Algae grow on the underside of the ice, and in summer a lot of plant plankton floats in the water.

The bearded seal uses its webbed feet like paddles to push against the water and help it swim along.

Amazing Adaptation

The bearded seal has good hearing to help it detect the tiny noises made by animals on the ocean floor and large eyes to see fish, such as Arctic cod, swimming in dimly-lit waters. It gets its name from the long, white, drooping whiskers on its face. These sensitive whiskers help it to feel around the ocean floor for crabs and shellfish to eat.

Bearded seals

Bearded seals, like polar bears and Adelie penguins, have dense waterproof fur and a thick layer of fat, called **blubber**, under their skin to keep warm in Arctic waters. Bearded seals dive to feed on the ocean floor under sheets of ice, but return to the surface to breathe. They use their hard heads to crash through thin ice to create breathing holes.

Icefish

Some fish in the Southern Ocean survive by living deep in its waters, because here the water stays at a more constant temperature and does not freeze. Icefish are one of the few types of fish that can live their whole lives in these icy waters. Their secret is their ability to make substances, nicknamed antifreeze, in their blood that lower the point at which the body freezes. It stops ice from growing inside the fish's body.

The ghostly-looking blackfin icefish has a large mouth with small teeth for grasping fish, crabs, and other prey that it catches near the ocean floor.

Fact Focus: Life in the Slow Lane

Most of the animals that live in frozen oceans live longer than similar animals in other oceans. The reason is that the cold temperatures slow everything down, so animals do everything at a much gentler pace, using less energy.

IN THE DEEP

A little light still reaches the ocean around 165 feet (50 m) below the water's surface, but 2,000 feet (600 m) down it is pitch black. Some strange and fearsome-looking animals call these depths home.

Deep-sea anglers

Deep-sea animals have developed some amazing ways of catching prey in the darkness. Some fish, octopuses, and squid have parts called photophores on their body. These contain **bacteria** that can produce light. Anglerfish get their name from angling, or fishing. A spine dangles a photophore near the anglerfish's mouth. The fish waves it back and forth like a fishing line to attract prey. When a fish gets close enough, the anglerfish grabs it in its needle-sharp teeth.

Amazing Adaptation

An angler fish can stretch its jaw and stomach to swallow prey twice the size of its body. This allows it to stock up on food when it can, since there are fewer fish to prey on in the deep sea.

An anglerfish has teeth that are angled inward, so its prey cannot escape once caught.

Deep-sea divers

Sperm whales dive as deep as 3,300 feet (1,000 m) hunting for prey, such as giant squid. To find prey in deep ocean waters where it is too dark to see, they use **echolocation**. First, they produce and send out clicking sounds. These spread out in the water and when they hit an animal, such as a squid, the sounds reflect, or bounce, back toward the whale.

The whale can find out where the prey is and how big it is by figuring out where the echoes are coming from and how long it takes for them to return.

Sperm whales hold their breath for up to 90 minutes when diving. Their 8-inch (20-cm) teeth weigh up to 2 pounds (1 kg) each and help them to eat about 2,200 pounds (1,000 kg) of fish and squid a day!

Fact File: The Mariana Trench

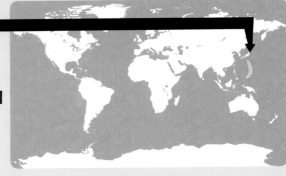

Location: The western Pacific Ocean
Size: 1,575 miles (2,540 km) long and 45 miles (70 km) wide at widest point and 7 miles (11 km) below **sea level** at its deepest point
Overview: The deepest point on Earth, this trench on the sea floor is deeper than Mount Everest is high.

OCEAN PREDATORS

The ocean is a dangerous place, where deadly predators use a variety of tactics to catch and eat other animals in the battle for survival.

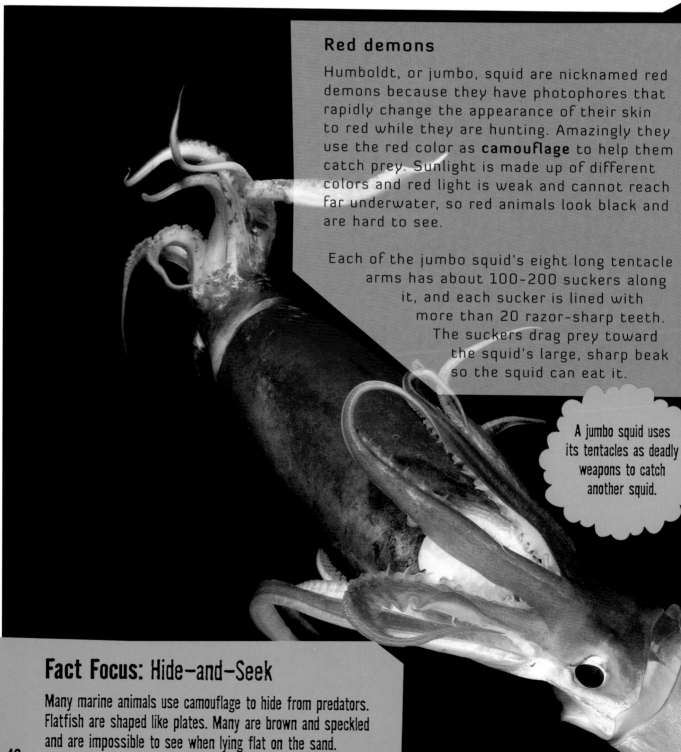

Red demons

Humboldt, or jumbo, squid are nicknamed red demons because they have photophores that rapidly change the appearance of their skin to red while they are hunting. Amazingly they use the red color as **camouflage** to help them catch prey. Sunlight is made up of different colors and red light is weak and cannot reach far underwater, so red animals look black and are hard to see.

Each of the jumbo squid's eight long tentacle arms has about 100-200 suckers along it, and each sucker is lined with more than 20 razor-sharp teeth. The suckers drag prey toward the squid's large, sharp beak so the squid can eat it.

A jumbo squid uses its tentacles as deadly weapons to catch another squid.

Fact Focus: Hide-and-Seek

Many marine animals use camouflage to hide from predators. Flatfish are shaped like plates. Many are brown and speckled and are impossible to see when lying flat on the sand.

Clever coloration

Many fish, whales, and dolphins have a dark back and a light belly. This is called countershading. When animals swimming below them look up, the light color of the belly blends in with light shining into the ocean from above. When animals swimming above them look down, their dark back blends in with the darkness below. Some prey animals use countershading to hide. Great white sharks use it as camouflage to sneak up on prey!

Amazing Adaptation

When sharks lose teeth in an attack, they simply grow new ones. A shark may lose and grow up to 30,000 teeth in its lifetime.

Great white sharks

A great white shark attack is sudden and vicious. The shark moves its tail fin side to side quickly to shoot up through the water. As it nears the surface it opens its mouth to snatch up prey as it bursts through the surface. It often kills prey with one huge bite.

The great white shark's huge mouth is full of razor-sharp teeth that can bite through skin, flesh, and bone of prey, such as seals, squid, and dolphins.

BORN SURVIVORS

Some ocean animals have amazing ways to make sure their eggs or young get the best start in life in the marine biome.

Seahorse fathers

Many fish scatter their eggs in the water, and the **larvae** that hatch get no help from their parents. Seahorses are different. The female seahorse places her 1,500 tiny eggs inside a pouch on the front of the male seahorse's body. The male seahorse keeps the eggs inside its pouch until they hatch to prevent them from being eaten by fish and other marine animals.

When the eggs are ready to hatch, the male seahorse opens the pouch, and the baby seahorses, known as fry, swim out into the sea.

Seahorse fry are about as big as your smallest fingernail. They look like miniature versions of their parents. Each fry eats about 3,000 bits of food per day.

Fact Focus: Egg Numbers

Fish lay thousands of eggs at once because so many larvae die before growing up. Less than one in a thousand seahorse fry become adults. The rest are eaten by predators or are washed away from their food supply by waves.

A nest of sand

Sea turtles feed, swim, and sleep in the ocean. Females travel hundreds of miles (kilometers) across the water each year to return to the beach where they were born and lay their eggs. They arrive at night and choose a dark, quiet spot. They use their flippers to dig a deep pit in the sand and lay up to 100 eggs inside it.

They cover the nest with damp sand and then kick dry sand on top to hide its location from predators. Then they return to the sea. The nest is a warm, safe place for the eggs.

Amazing Adaptation

Sea turtles have long paddle-shaped flippers for swimming, but these flippers also make handy spades to help the females dig holes in the sand.

After two months, the sea turtle babies hatch. They dig themselves out of the sand and crawl as fast as they can to the sea, before hungry birds snap them up.

EAT OR BE EATEN

The lives of all marine plants and animals are linked together in different **food chains**. Food chains tell the story of how food energy is passed from plants to animals.

From phytoplankton to blue whales

Plants are the first link in a food chain, as they make their own food using sunlight in the process of photosynthesis. Tiny plants in plankton are called phytoplankton. Phytoplankton are flat and round or have spines or hairs that help them float near the surface to get light.

Phytoplankton are eaten by shrimp-like animals called krill that swim using five pairs of tiny legs. In the Southern Ocean, krill live in huge swarms that may have 20,000 krill per cubic yard (26,000 krill per cubic meter). They are easy prey for blue whales, which are the next link in this particular food chain.

Krill swim toward the surface of the water during the night to look for food and back down into the ocean during the day to try to avoid predators.

Amazing Adaptation

Baleen whales, such as the blue whale, use their tongues to push water through fringed plates inside their mouths that filter tons of krill from the seawater.

From seaweed to sea otters

Some ocean food chains begin with seaweed. Sea snails eat seaweed and are eaten by crabs, which are eaten by seabirds.

Kelp is a type of seaweed eaten by sea urchins. These small, spiky marine animals have a beak-like mouth for grinding up the seaweed. Sea urchins are eaten by sea otters. Sea otters have a wide flat tail they move up and down and webbed feet that help them dive to catch the sea urchins. Their paws have rough pads for grabbing prey.

A sea otter lays on its back at the surface and uses its belly as a dining table while it tucks into its prey. Most sea otters use their paws to break the prickly spines off the sea urchins before they eat them!

Fact Focus: Food Webs

Several food chains connected together form **food webs**. For example, animal plankton is eaten by cod and seals. Sea stars are eaten by whales. Cod is eaten by whales and seals. Seals are eaten by polar bears.

OCEANS AND PEOPLE

All of us depend on the oceans. People travel or carry goods around the world in huge ships, and they sail and swim in marine biomes for fun. Oceans and seas also provide food, oil, medicines, and other substances that we use every day.

From the sea to the shops

Fish and shellfish are an important food source for millions of people. Catching, preparing, and selling these fish provide millions more with jobs. People also catch krill to make animal feed and use seaweed to make products such as ice cream and toothpaste smooth and creamy.

Scuba divers wear oxygen tanks so they can enjoy swimming underwater with amazing marine wildlife such as this huge manta ray.

Fact Focus: Overfishing

People are taking fish out of the ocean faster than fish can reproduce and replenish their populations. This means that some, such as bluefin tuna, are in danger of **extinction**.

Ocean pharmacies

Marine biomes may not look like your local pharmacist, but they are an important source of medicines. Scientists make copies of chemicals they find in living things, such as sponges and corals, and use these copies to develop medicines. Sea squirts have helped make a cancer medicine, and a cone snail has been used to make a painkiller.

The ocean floor

People dig up useful resources from beneath the ocean floor. They drill for oil, which is used as a fuel and to make electricity. It's also used to make plastics, **fertilizers**, fabrics, and many other products. Sand and gravel are used in buildings. Metals such as copper are used in mobile phones, and titanium is used in aircraft.

Sea squirts like this one have been used to make a cancer drug. Sea squirts are so named because they squirt water when removed from the ocean, probably as a form of self-defense!

Fact Focus: Oxygen Supply

The oceans help to give us the air we breathe! Phytoplanktons produce about 70 percent of Earth's oxygen. They release it as waste when they make their food by photosynthesis.

MARINE THREATS

Accidentally or on purpose, people dump all sorts of waste into oceans and seas. This **pollution** puts marine biomes and their wildlife in danger.

Pollution problems

Most marine pollution is solid waste, such as fishing nets and plastic bags. Then there are the dirt and chemicals that are washed down drains from bathrooms or farm fields. Ships sometimes leak or spill oil into oceans when they are damaged.

Oil spills clog fur and feathers, stopping birds and animals from keeping warm. Other animals are injured or killed by rubbish, because they become entangled in it or mistake it for food.

Many sea turtles die each year because they mistake floating plastic bags for the jellyfish they like to eat.

Fact Focus: The Power of Plastic

Plastic floats and takes hundreds of years to decompose. Birds starve when their stomachs are full of plastic waste, and plastic kills many thousands of other marine animals each year.

Global warming

The gradual rise in world temperatures from **global warming** is making seas and oceans warmer. Krill need freezing cold water to **breed**, so there are fewer krill for fish, seals, and whales to eat.

Coral polyps share food with the algae that live among them, but algae cannot make food by photosynthesis in very warm water, so they die. This weakens and kills corals, robbing other reef animals of the food and shelter they need in order to survive.

As oceans get warmer, some animals move to parts of the marine biome where it was too cold for them before. Without natural enemies in these places, they are free to devour anything in their path.

Because of the increase in ocean temperatures, thousands of giant king crabs have invaded the deep Southern Ocean, where they are killing huge numbers of sea urchins, sea stars, and other wildlife.

MARINE FUTURES

Oceans and seas are beautiful natural biomes full of amazing wildlife, and they provide us with many useful resources. It is vital to protect them for the future.

Laws and rules

Many countries have laws to stop people from releasing dangerous waste into oceans. There are laws to regulate fishing areas and which fish can be caught to prevent overfishing. Laws also stop the hunting of **endangered** animals, such as walruses.

Marine reserves

Marine reserves are areas of water protected by law, where fishing and mining are banned and the number of people who can visit is limited.

Hawaiian monk seals are an endangered animal, but many now live safely in the Papahānaumokuākea marine reserve.

Fact File: The Papahānaumokuākea Marine National Monument

Location: The Pacific Ocean around the northwestern islands of Hawaii
Size: 582,000 sq. mi. (1,507,770 km²)
Overview: Biggest marine reserve in the world and home to the world's healthiest coral reefs and blue whales, sea turtles, and Hawaiian monk seals.

Conservation helps

Some conservation workers rescue injured or ill animals or clean up seabirds after an oil spill. Others study ocean biomes to find out what the problems are and what can be done to help. They inform people about dangers facing marine biomes so that more people get involved in protecting them.

What you can do

You can help marine biomes by reducing waste. Buy reusable items such as water bottles and recycle things such as cans and mobile phones. Avoid dropping litter, especially near waterways. Look out for opportunities to help on a beach clean-up at a body of water near you or when on holiday. You could also support a **conservation** group that works to protect coasts, oceans, and seas.

Follow the seashore code at the coast. Take care when looking in rock pools. Turn rocks gently and put them back where you found them so you don't destroy animal homes.

Fact Focus: Wind and Wave Power

Burning coal to make electricity is one cause of global warming. In some oceans, people build power stations that make electricity using wave or wind power instead of **fossil fuels**. This reduces the pollution that causes global warming.

GLOSSARY

adaptation Special feature or way of behaving that helps a living thing survive in its habitat

algae Plant-like living things that grow in damp places

bacteria Tiny living things that can cause diseases or decompose waste

biome Large region of Earth with living things adapted to the typical climate, soils, and other features

blubber Thick layer of fat beneath the skin of some animals

breed to have young or babies

camouflage Colors and patterns that help hide an animal's body against its surroundings

climate Typical weather pattern through the year in an area

conservation The act of guarding, protecting or preserving something

continent One of seven large masses of land: Asia, Africa, North America, South America, Europe, Australia, and Antarctica

dissolved Mixed with a liquid so it becomes part of the liquid

echolocation Way of finding things using echoes that bounce off objects

endangered At risk of dying out

equator Imaginary line around the center of the Earth

extinction When every plant or animal of a particular kind has died out.

fertilizer A substance added to soil to help plants grow

filter To pass something through tiny holes to remove unwanted material

flippers Wide, flat limb (arm or leg) used for swimming

food chain A way of showing the movement of the sun's energy from one living thing to another

food web A network of related food chains that show how energy is passed from one living thing to another.

fossil fuels Natural fuel, such as coal or gas, formed from the remains of living things

friction The force that makes a moving object slow down when it rubs against another

frond Leaf-like parts found on seaweed.

gills Body parts that fish and some other animals use to breathe underwater

global warming Rise in average temperature of Earth caused by human use of machines and electricity that is altering weather patterns worldwide

habitat Place where an animal or plant lives.

holdfast Part of a seaweed that anchors it to rocks

kidneys Body parts that remove waste products from the blood

larvae Animals at the stage when they have just hatched out of their eggs

limestone Hard sedimentary rock

mollusk Animal with a soft body that is usually covered with a shell

organs Parts of the body, such as heart and lungs, that perform specific functions

photosynthesis Process by which green plants make sugary food using energy in sunlight.

plankton Microscopic plants and animals that float in oceans and seas

pollution Something that damages water, air, or land or makes it harmful to living things

predator Animal that eats other animals

prey Animal eaten by another animal

sea level The level of the surface of oceans and seas

seaweed A plant-like living thing found in marine biomes

streamlined Shaped to move more easily through air or water

tentacles Long, flexible animal arms

tide The rise and fall of water along ocean coasts

tropics Warm region surrounding the equator

urine Liquid waste material secreted by animals

FIND OUT MORE

Books

Oceans Inside Out (Ecosystems Inside Out)
Robin Johnson
Crabtree Publishing, 2015

Ultimate Oceanpedia: The Most Complete Ocean Reference Ever
Christina Wilsdon
National Geographic Children's Books, 2016

Ocean Animals: Who's Who in the Deep Blue
Johnna Rizzo
National Geographic Children's Books, 2016

Earth's Oceans (Where's the Water?)
Peter Castellano
Gareth Stevens Publishing, 2016

Websites

There are games, facts, and pictures about oceans at this
World Wildlife Fund site:

gowild.wwf.org.uk/oceans

Watch a video about the deep part of the ocean at PBS Learning:
http://bit.ly/2AXq2hW

Watch ocean videos at:

www.bbc.co.uk/science/earth/water_and_ice/ocean

Find out how to stop ocean pollution at:

www.greenpeace.org/usa/oceans/preventing-pollution/

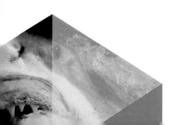

INDEX